ULTIMATE SPORTS STATS

PRO BASKETBALL BY THE NUMBERS

Percy Leed

Lerner Publications ◆ Minneapolis

Stats are accurate through the 2022–2023 NBA regular season.
Stats are accurate through the 2023 WNBA regular season.

Lerner Publications Company
An imprint of Lerner Publishing Group, Inc.
241 First Avenue North
Minneapolis, MN 55401 USA

For reading levels and more information, look up this title at www.lernerbooks.com.

Main body text set in Adrianna.
Typeface provided by Chank.

Designer: Viet Chu
Lerner team: Sue Marquis

Library of Congress Cataloging-in-Publication Data

Names: Leed, Percy, 1968– author.
Title: Pro basketball by the numbers / Percy Leed.
Description: Minneapolis, MN : Lerner Publications, [2025] | Series: Lerner sports. Ultimate sports stats | Includes bibliographical references and index. | Audience: Ages 7–11 | Audience: Grades 2–3 | Summary: “Which basketball teams are rising to the top? Which players are the best passers and scorers of all time? Basketball stats give the answers to these and many more questions. Explore the most exciting basketball stats of all time”— Provided by publisher.
Identifiers: LCCN 2023045505 (print) | LCCN 2023045506 (ebook) | ISBN 9798765625934 (library binding) | ISBN 9798765629864 (paperback) | ISBN 9798765638125 (epub)
Subjects: LCSH: Basketball—Statistics—Juvenile literature. | Basketball—Records—Juvenile literature.
Classification: LCC GV885.1 .L453 2025 (print) | LCC GV885.1 (ebook) | DDC 796.323—dc23/eng/20231019

LC record available at https://lccn.loc.gov/2023045505
LC ebook record available at https://lccn.loc.gov/2023045506

Manufactured in the United States of America
1-1010066-51927-2/20/2024

TABLE OF CONTENTS

INTRODUCTION

PEACH BASKETS

On December 21, 1891, a teacher named James Naismith showed his class a new game. Naismith brought his class to a gym and split them into two teams. Each end of the gym had a peach basket. Players tried to get the ball from the other team. They then threw it into one of the baskets to earn points. Naismith had invented the game of basketball.

Basketball stories can be told through stats. Fans use stats to keep track of how well players and teams do. Teams use stats to learn about their opponents. Stats can help teams figure out how to win. To understand basketball stats, you need to know how the rules of the game have changed over time.

DR. JAMES NAISMITH

A SLOWER GAME

At first, basketball games often had low scores. Games moved slowly. The baskets had bottoms. Each time a shot went in, someone had to climb a ladder to get the ball. Baskets with open bottoms were not used until 1912.

Games were also slow because teams would often stop shooting once they took the lead. They did this so the other team would have fewer chances to score. In 1954, the National Basketball Association (NBA) began to use a 24-second shot clock. This forced teams to shoot more often and score more points. A year later, the Boston Celtics became the first team to average at least 100 points per game for a season.

WOMEN BEGAN PLAYING BASKETBALL SOON AFTER THE GAME WAS INVENTED.

WAIT, WHAT!?

In the first basketball game, the players used a soccer ball. The game lasted 30 minutes. William R. Chase scored the game's first basket.

CHAPTER 1

PLAYER STATS

GAME TIME

An NBA team plays 82 games each regular season. But most NBA players don't play every game. Some only play for a few minutes per game. You can check a player's stats to know how much they have really played.

KAREEM ABDUL-JABBAR

MOST MINUTES PLAYED IN AN NBA CAREER

PLAYER	MINUTES PLAYED
Kareem Abdul-Jabbar	57,446
Karl Malone	54,852
LeBron James	54,093
Dirk Nowitzki	51,368
Kevin Garnett	50,418

MAKING HISTORY

For many years, Kareem Abdul-Jabbar was the NBA's leader in career points scored. He has won more MVP awards than anyone else. He was great in college too. He scored 56 points in his first varsity game. In 2023, LeBron James broke his NBA record for career points scored.

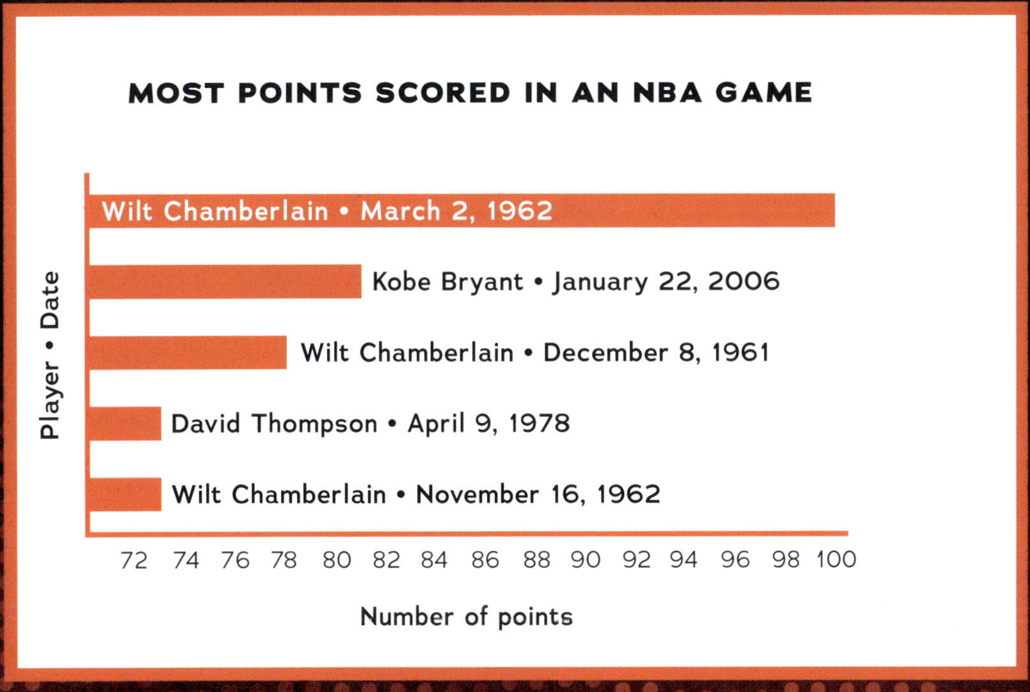

WAIT, WHAT!?

Few NBA players have scored 60 points or more in multiple games. Kobe Bryant did it six times. Wilt Chamberlain did it 32 times!

Diana Taurasi

Diana Taurasi was a great scorer from the start. She joined the Women's National Basketball Association (WNBA) in 2004 and scored 22 points in her first game. In 2017, Taurasi overtook Tina Thompson's record of 7,488 career points. Taurasi became the WNBA's all-time best scorer.

DIANA TAURASI

HIGHEST SCORING AVERAGE PER GAME IN A WNBA SEASON

PLAYER	TEAM	SEASON	POINTS
Diana Taurasi	Phoenix Mercury	2006	25.3
Jewell Loyd	Seattle Storm	2023	24.7
Diana Taurasi	Phoenix Mercury	2008	24.1
Maya Moore	Minnesota Lynx	2014	23.9
Lauren Jackson	Seattle Storm	2007	23.8

SCORING SPECIALISTS

Scoring is one of the most important stats to fans and teams. The greatest scorers in the NBA all had something special. To score a lot of points, players need a shot that is hard to block. Kareem Abdul-Jabbar had his special move, the skyhook. Michael Jordan could jump high to score over people's heads. Kobe Bryant could score from anywhere on the court.

KOBE BRYANT

MOST NBA CAREER POINTS SCORED

PLAYER	POINTS
LeBron James	38,652
Kareem Abdul-Jabbar	38,387
Karl Malone	36,928
Kobe Bryant	33,643
Michael Jordan	32,292

INSTANT SUCCESS

The WNBA had its first season in 1997. It started with eight teams. By 2000, the league had doubled in size to include 16 teams. The league's first draft pick, Tina Thompson, played for 17 seasons. Thompson was the league's all-time scoring leader until Diana Taurasi passed her.

MOST WNBA CAREER POINTS SCORED

PLAYER	POINTS
Diana Taurasi	10,108
Tina Thompson	7,488
Tamika Catchings	7,380
Tina Charles	7,115
Candice Dupree	6,895

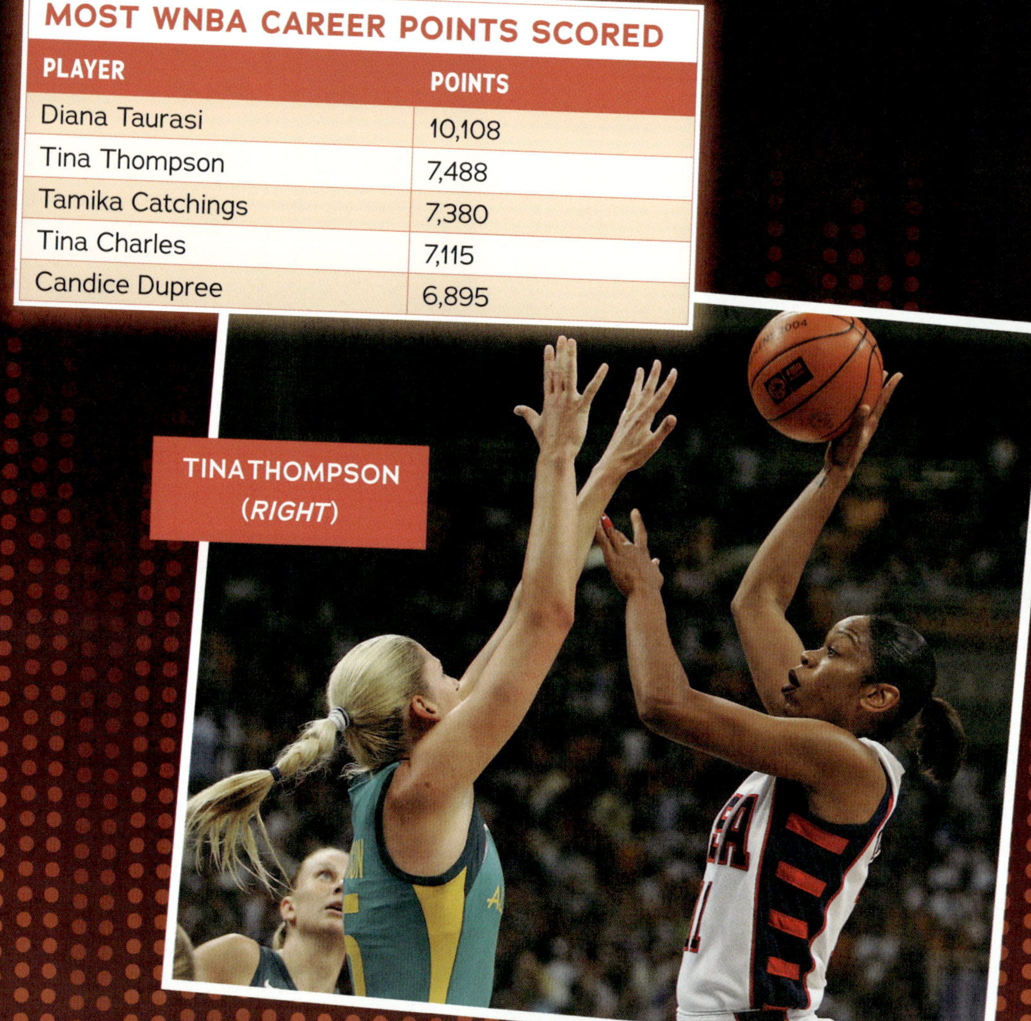

TINA THOMPSON (*RIGHT*)

THREE-POINT SHOTS

Chris Ford of the Boston Celtics made the first three-pointer in NBA history on October 12, 1979. Players soon followed his lead. Many started to specialize in shooting three-pointers. Shooting three-pointers is a way for a team to score a lot of points quickly.

MOST THREE-POINTERS IN AN NBA SEASON

PLAYER	TEAM	SEASON	THREE-POINTERS
Stephen Curry	Golden State Warriors	2015–2016	402
James Harden	Philadelphia 76ers	2018–2019	378
Stephen Curry	Golden State Warriors	2018–2019	354
Stephen Curry	Golden State Warriors	2020–2021	337
Stephen Curry	Golden State Warriors	2016–2017	324

STEPHEN CURRY

MOST THREE-POINTERS IN AN NBA CAREER

PLAYER	THREE-POINTERS
Stephen Curry	3,390
Ray Allen	2,973
James Harden	2,754
Reggie Miller	2,560
Kyle Korver	2,450

GRABBING THE REBOUND

Players often miss shots. But another player can grab the ball for a rebound. Good rebounding teams have a big advantage.

Wilt Chamberlain is the all-time leading rebounder with 23,924 rebounds. Boston Celtics player Bill Russell is right behind him with 21,620. Both players were tall. They towered over other players on the court. This gave Chamberlain and Russell an advantage at getting rebounds.

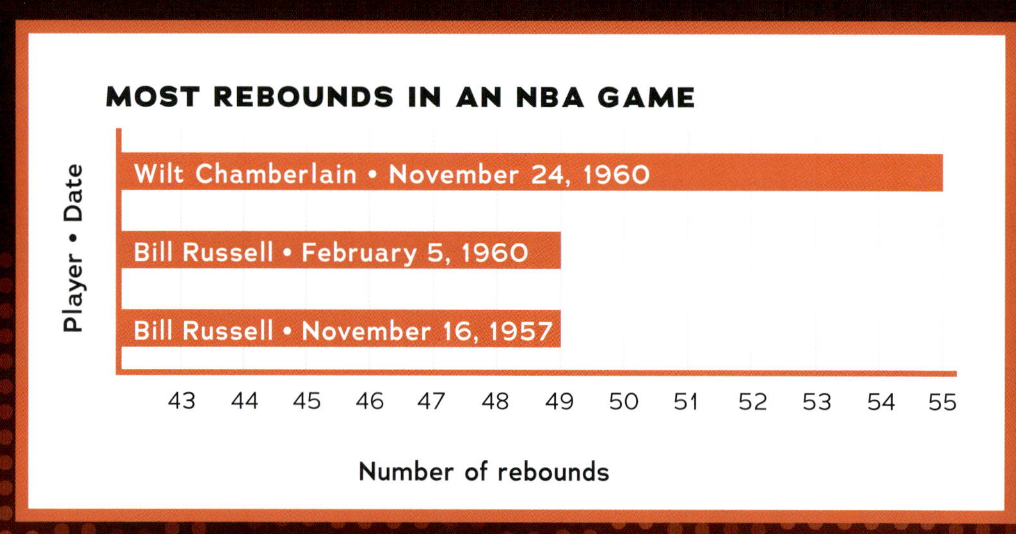

WAIT, WHAT!?

Many fans call Michael Jordan the greatest basketball player of all time. He won the MVP award five times. He won the NBA championship six times!

MICHAEL JORDAN

Another way to get the ball is to steal it. A steal happens when a player takes the ball from a player on the other team. Players who are good at stealing are usually guards, who are often small and quick.

MOST NBA CAREER STEALS

PLAYER	STEALS
John Stockton	3,265
Jason Kidd	2,684
Chris Paul	2,544
Michael Jordan	2,514
Gary Payton Sr.	2,445

JASON KIDD (*RIGHT*)

WAIT, WHAT!?

The NBA did not start recording steals as an official stat until the 1973–1974 season. The first season leader in steals was Larry Steele.

THE BEST BLOCKERS

Players usually jump when they shoot. But opponents can also jump to block their shot. The greatest blockers were tall. Hakeem Olajuwon stood 7 feet (2.1 m) tall. He is the all-time leader in blocked shots.

HAKEEM OLAJUWON (*CENTER*)

MOST BLOCKS IN AN NBA CAREER

PLAYER	HEIGHT	BLOCKS
Hakeem Olajuwon	7' (2.1 m)	3,830
Dikembe Mutombo	7'2" (2.2 m)	3,289
Kareem Abdul-Jabbar	7'2" (2.2 m)	3,189
Mark Eaton	7'4" (2.2 m)	3,064

MOST BLOCKS IN AN NBA GAME

PLAYER	HEIGHT	BLOCKS	DATE
Elmore Smith	7' (2.1 m)	17	October 28, 1973
Shaquille O'Neal	7'1" (2.1 m)	15	November 20, 1993
Manute Bol	7'7" (2.3 m)	15	February 26, 1987
Manute Bol	7'7" (2.3 m)	15	January 25, 1986

THE TRIPLE-DOUBLE

Basketball fans often focus on five main stats. These are points, rebounds, assists, steals, and blocked shots. Reaching double digits (10 or more) in three different stats is called a triple-double. Triple-doubles are rare. In an amazing 1961–1962 season, Oscar Robertson of the Cincinnati Royals averaged a triple-double (30.8 points, 11.4 assists, and 12.5 rebounds) for the entire season! It took 55 years for another player, Russell Westbrook, to break Robertson's record.

RUSSELL WESTBROOK

MOST TRIPLE-DOUBLES IN AN NBA SEASON

PLAYER	SEASON	TRIPLE-DOUBLES
Russell Westbrook	2016–2017	42
Oscar Robertson	1961–1962	41
Russell Westbrook	2020–2021	38
Russell Westbrook	2018–2019	34
Wilt Chamberlain	1967–1968	31

BEST OF THE BEST

The NBA MVP award has been given to the best player of the regular season since 1956. Until 1980, players voted to decide the best player. In 1981, a group of sportswriters and sports broadcasters began choosing the winner. The trophy has been awarded 67 times, but only 35 players have won it. Many players have won the trophy several times.

KAREEM ABDUL-JABBAR

TOP NBA MVP WINNERS

MVP AWARDS	PLAYER	MVP SEASONS
6	Kareem Abdul-Jabbar	1971, 1972, 1974, 1976, 1977, 1980
5	Michael Jordan	1988, 1991, 1992, 1996, 1998
5	Bill Russell	1958, 1961, 1962, 1963, 1965
4	LeBron James	2009, 2010, 2012, 2013
4	Wilt Chamberlain	1960, 1966, 1967, 1968

WAIT, WHAT!?

In 2016, Golden State Warriors player Stephen Curry became the only NBA player to win the MVP trophy in a unanimous vote. That means he was every voter's first choice.

CHAPTER 2

TEAM STATS

WINNING SUPER STATS

The Los Angeles Sparks joined the WNBA in 1997, the league's first season. Since then, the Sparks have appeared in 20 playoffs and won three championships. They have won a higher percentage of their games than any other team that has been in the league since 1997.

LAYSHIA CLARENDON (*CENTER LEFT*) WITH THE 2023 LOS ANGELES SPARKS

BEST WNBA WINNING PERCENTAGES

TEAM	GAMES PLAYED	GAMES WON	WINNING PERCENTAGE
Los Angeles Sparks	894	522	.584
New York Liberty	894	450	.503
Phoenix Mercury	894	449	.502
Las Vegas Aces	894	428	.479

BREAKING RECORDS

In 2015–2016, the Golden State Warriors had their best season yet. They won game after game. On the last day of the regular season, they overtook the win total set by the Chicago Bulls 20 years earlier. The Warriors went 73–9 in the regular season. It was the best regular-season record in NBA history.

BEST NBA REGULAR-SEASON RECORDS

YEAR	TEAM	RECORD
2015–2016	Golden State Warriors	73–9
1995–1996	Chicago Bulls	72–10
1996–1997	Chicago Bulls	69–13
1971–1972	Los Angeles Lakers	69–13
1966–1967	Philadelphia 76ers	68–13

GOLDEN STATE WARRIORS PLAYERS IN 2015–2016

WINNING THE TROPHY

Every year, a WNBA team wins the championship trophy. Players work hard to help their team win it. In 1997, the Houston Comets started a winning streak that did not end until 2000. They played in every championship for four years and won each time.

WAIT, WHAT!?

In 2023, the Las Vegas Aces won the WNBA championship for the second year in a row. They became the first team to win back-to-back WNBA championships in more than 20 years.

WINNING STREAKS

Sometimes a team just can't stop winning! The Los Angeles Lakers won 33 games in a row in the 1971–1972 season. It was the longest winning streak ever in a major pro team sport. The Miami Heat came close to the record in the 2012–2013 season with 27 games. The Golden State Warriors started their 2015–2016 season with 24 wins before breaking their streak.

MOST WINS IN A ROW IN AN NBA SEASON

TEAM	FIRST GAME OF STREAK	LAST GAME OF STREAK	GAMES WON
Los Angeles Lakers	November 5, 1971	January 7, 1972	33
Miami Heat	February 3, 2013	March 27, 2013	27
Golden State Warriors	October 27, 2015	December 12, 2015	24

ANDRE IGUODALA DRIBBLES THE BALL FOR THE GOLDEN STATE WARRIORS IN 2015–2016.

BIGGEST WINS

In 1991, the Cleveland Cavaliers played against the Miami Heat. Miami had beaten them by two points a week earlier, and the Cavaliers weren't about to let the Heat win again. The Cavaliers were up by 20 points at halftime. They went on to win 148–80. The game had the biggest score difference in NBA history until the Memphis Grizzlies and Oklahoma City Thunder topped it in 2021–2022.

BIGGEST SCORE DIFFERENCES IN AN NBA GAME

DATE	WINNING TEAM	LOSING TEAM	SCORE
December 2, 2021	Memphis Grizzlies	Oklahoma City Thunder	152–79
December 17, 1991	Cleveland Cavaliers	Miami Heat	148–80
February 27, 1998	Indiana Pacers	Portland Trail Blazers	124–59
March 19, 1972	Los Angeles Lakers	Golden State Warriors	162–99
November 2, 1991	Golden State Warriors	Sacramento Kings	153–91

SANTI ALDAMA (*LEFT*) OF THE MEMPHIS GRIZZLIES PLAYING AGAINST THE OKLAHOMA CITY THUNDER

PLAYOFF TEAMS

In 1975–1976, the Detroit Pistons had a losing record, yet they still made the playoffs. Then they won their first playoff series two games to one. Their opponent, the Milwaukee Bucks, also had a losing record. No team with a losing record has ever won a playoff series again.

BOB LANIER (*LEFT*) WITH THE 1975–1976 DETROIT PISTONS

MOST NBA PLAYOFF APPEARANCES

TEAM	PLAYOFF APPEARANCES
Los Angeles Lakers	63
Boston Celtics	60
Philadelphia 76ers	53
Atlanta Hawks	49
San Antonio Spurs	47

CHAPTER 3

STATS ARE HERE TO STAY

THE BOX SCORE

A box score is a chart that contains stats from a game. By looking at a box score, fans can find out everything they want to know about that game. In the 2023 NBA Finals, the Denver Nuggets defeated the Miami Heat in five games. On the next page, use the key to read the Denver box score from the last game of the Finals.

NIKOLA JOKIĆ

KEY
REB = rebounds
AST = assists
STL = steals
BLK = blocks
PTS = points

DENVER NUGGETS

STARTERS	REB	AST	STL	BLK	PTS
Nikola Jokić	16	4	0	1	28
Jamal Murray	8	8	1	0	14
Kentavious Caldwell-Pope	4	2	2	3	11
Michael Porter Jr.	13	3	0	0	16
Aaron Gordon	7	1	2	1	4
RESERVES	**REB**	**AST**	**STL**	**BLK**	**PTS**
Bruce Brown	6	1	1	0	10
Christian Braun	3	1	0	1	7
Jeff Green	0	1	0	0	4
DeAndre Jordan	0	0	0	1	0

DENVER NUGGETS PLAYERS CELEBRATE THEIR WIN IN THE 2023 NBA FINALS.

HEAD COACH BECKY HAMMON (*LEFT*) TALKS WITH LAS VEGAS ACES PLAYERS IN 2023.

STATS AND STRATEGY

Stats aren't only read by fans who love the game. Players and coaches also read stats to help them perform better. One way players use stats is to plan ways to guard opponents. For instance, if a player is great at making three-pointers, the opposing team will guard that player more closely at the three-point line.

CHANGING THE GAME

Stats continue to change the game. In recent seasons, coaches noticed that winning teams often attempted more three-point shots than losing teams did. So coaches began asking players to take more long shots. It will be fun to see how stats continue to affect the game in seasons to come.

STATS MATCHUP

Stephen Curry was the NBA MVP in 2014–2015 and 2015–2016. He has led his Golden State Warriors to four titles and came within moments of winning another before losing to LeBron James and his Cleveland Cavaliers.

STEPHEN CURRY GOLDEN STATE WARRIORS	
Points	1,648
Three-pointers made	273
Rebounds	341
Assists	352
Steals	52

STEPHEN CURRY

James has been the league MVP four times, and his teams have won four titles. Here are the superstars' stats for the 2022–2023 season. Who is the greater player? You decide.

LEBRON JAMES CLEVELAND CAVALIERS	
Points	1,590
Three-pointers made	121
Rebounds	457
Assists	375
Steals	50

LEBRON JAMES

GLOSSARY

blocked shot: a defensive play in which the ball is knocked away by a defender before reaching the hoop

career: a profession, such as athlete

draft: when teams take turns choosing new players

MVP: short for *most valuable player*

rebound: grabbing and controlling the ball after a missed shot

shot clock: a 24-second timer that begins as soon as a team gets the ball. If a team doesn't hit the backboard or rim with a shot within 24 seconds, the other team takes the ball.

steal: when a player takes the ball from a player on the other team

three-point line: a line on a basketball court beyond which making a basket counts for three points

Learn More

Brittanica Kids: Basketball
https://kids.britannica.com/kids/article/basketball/352831

Fishman, Jon M. *Tina Charles vs. Lisa Leslie: Who Would Win?* Minneapolis: Lerner Publications, 2024.

Kawa, Katie. *Stephen Curry: Making a Difference as a Basketball Champion*. Buffalo: KidHaven, 2024.

Kiddle: Basketball Facts for Kids
https://kids.kiddle.co/Basketball

Kiddle: Women's National Basketball Association Facts for Kids
https://kids.kiddle.co/Women%27s_National_Basketball_Association

Whiting, Jim. *The Story of the Seattle Storm*. Mankato, MN: Creative Education and Creative Paperbacks, 2024.

INDEX

PHOTO ACKNOWLEDGMENTS

Image credits: Bettmann/Getty Images, pp. 4, 17; ullstein bild Dtl./Getty Images, p. 5; Focus On Sport/Getty Images, pp. 6, 15; Icon Sportswire/Getty Images, p. 8; Stephen Dunn/Getty Images, p. 9; Doug Pensinger/Getty Images, p. 10; Ezra Shaw/Getty Images, p. 11; Jamie Squire/Getty Images, p. 13; Marc Serota/Stringer/Getty Images, p. 14; Dustin Satloff/Getty Images, p. 16; Ethan Miller/Getty Images, pp. 18, 26; Jason Miller/Stringer/Getty Images, p. 19; Rich Schultz/Stringer/Getty Images, p. 21; AP Photo/Brandon Dill, p. 22; Paul Natkin/Getty Images, p. 23; Mike Ehrmann/Getty Images, p. 24; Justin Edmonds/Stringer/Getty Images, p. 25; SDI Productions/Getty Images/Getty Images, p. 27; Thearon W. Henderson/Getty Images, pp. 28–29.

Design elements: Ali Kahfi/Getty Images; sarayut Thaneerat/Getty Images.

Cover: AP Photo/Elaine Thompson.